Original title:
Joyful Moments

Copyright © 2024 Creative Arts Management OÜ
All rights reserved.

Author: Tim Wood
ISBN HARDBACK: 978-9916-88-226-9
ISBN PAPERBACK: 978-9916-88-227-6

Chasing Rainbows on a Tuesday

Under clouds painted gray and white,
We chase the colors, pure delight.
With each step, the puddles gleam,
A day that feels like a waking dream.

The sky opens wide, a canvas bright,
As rainbows dance in playful flight.
With laughter echoing, we run free,
Embracing the joy, just you and me.

Sweet Serenades of the Heart

In quiet moments, whispers rise,
Soft melodies beneath the skies.
A heartbeat chimes like ancient song,
Reminding us where we belong.

With each note, our souls entwine,
In harmony, your heart beats with mine.
A lullaby of dreams and chance,
In this sweet serenade, we dance.

Laughter in the Breeze

The wind carries giggles, light and clear,
As joy escapes, we draw it near.
Under the sun, we spin and sway,
Finding laughter in the day.

Every moment, a treasure found,
In playful whispers swirling around.
With every breeze, our spirits rise,
Chasing shadows beneath the skies.

Embers of Exuberance

In twilight's glow, the embers spark,
A fire ignites, chasing the dark.
With every flicker, dreams take flight,
Exhilaration in the night.

We gather close, hearts ablaze,
Sharing stories in vibrant rays.
In the warmth, we find our place,
Embers of joy, a sweet embrace.

Enchanted by the Little Things

A fluttering leaf in the breeze,
Whispers of magic among the trees.
A flower peeks through the soft earth,
Celebrating life, its quiet birth.

The sound of children's laughter rings,
Innocent joy that truly sings.
A evening star begins to glow,
Reminding us of all we know.

Serenade of the Simple

A warm cup shared in morning light,
Gentle moments that feel just right.
The scent of rain on thirsty ground,
In each small joy, love can be found.

A friend's embrace, a soft goodbye,
The way the clouds drift in the sky.
Every heartbeat, every sigh,
Paint the canvas of our why.

Sparkles in the Everyday

Morning dew on blades of grass,
Sunlight dances as moments pass.
A book's embrace, where stories thrive,
In every page, our dreams arrive.

The laughter shared over a meal,
In simple joy, our souls can heal.
A walk that stirs the heart awake,
In every step, new trails we make.

The Warmth of Shared Moments

A glance that sparks a hidden flame,
Love's whispers, soft and yet untamed.
A sunset painting skies of gold,
In each shared moment, warmth unfolds.

The comfort found in silence shared,
Trusting hearts, always prepared.
A story told by an open fire,
Kindred spirits lifting higher.

Tides of Contentment

Waves gently roll on sand so fine,
Sunlit whispers in a perfect line.
Footprints linger, washed away,
Time drifts softly, here we stay.

Heartbeats echo with the sea,
In this moment, just you and me.
Stars above in evening's glow,
In quiet peace, our spirits flow.

Days Spent in Harmony

Morning light spills through the trees,
A gentle song carried by the breeze.
Laughter dances on the air,
In each heartbeat, we find care.

Afternoon fades, golden and warm,
Together we weather every storm.
Shadows lengthen, the sun dips low,
In our hearts, the love will grow.

The Color of Shared Glances

Eyes meet softly, the world feels right,
A silent promise in fading light.
Colors swirl in a vibrant tune,
Hearts entwined beneath the moon.

Every smile, a story told,
In your gaze, a warmth unfolds.
Locked in moments, time stands still,
With each glance, we feel the thrill.

Butterflies in the Garden

A soft breeze flutters through the blooms,
Whispers of color in sunlit rooms.
Butterflies dance on petals bright,
Nature's beauty, pure delight.

In the garden, time unfolds,
Stories woven with dreams untold.
In their flight, a silent song,
In this space, we all belong.

Heartbeats of Happiness

In the morning's golden light,
Joyful whispers take their flight.
Every smile, a spark divine,
In the rhythm, hearts entwine.

Beneath the azure sky so clear,
Laughter dances, drawing near.
Together, we embrace the day,
As love's sweet melody will play.

Petals in a Gentle Wind

Softly drifting through the air,
Petals twirl without a care.
Colors blend, a vibrant sight,
Nature's brush in pure delight.

On the breeze, they sing a song,
Carried where the hearts belong.
In the stillness, peace we find,
Whispers shared with every kind.

Laughter Beneath the Stars

Underneath the starry dome,
Hearts find warmth, they're not alone.
Laughter rings like silver chimes,
Filling up the endless times.

In the night, dreams intertwine,
Every story, a precious sign.
Together we explore the night,
Bound by love, in pure delight.

Embracing Whimsy

In a world of colors bright,
Let the whimsy take its flight.
Chasing dreams on clouds of cheer,
Every moment, crystal clear.

Through the meadows, laughter flows,
In the dance where pure love grows.
Embrace the joy, no need to hide,
With hearts as one, we'll turn the tide.

Radiance in a Child's Gaze

Innocent wonder, bright and clear,
Sparkling eyes filled with cheer,
Dreams take flight on gentle wings,
In their gaze, the hope of springs.

Laughter dances on the breeze,
Joyful hearts at perfect ease,
Each small moment, pure delight,
Shining love, a guiding light.

Sunbeams Through the Leaves

Golden rays through branches play,
Nature whispers, 'Come and stay,'
Dappled light on forest floor,
A tranquil peace that we adore.

Rustling leaves in soft embrace,
Sunlight warms each hidden space,
Gentle beams like tender touch,
In this haven, we feel much.

A Garden of Gleaming Hearts

Blooms of color, bright and bold,
Whispers of the tales untold,
Petals soft, a sweet perfume,
In this space, the hearts find room.

Butterflies in graceful flight,
Dancing through the warm daylight,
Every blossom, a work of art,
In this garden, there's warm heart.

Bubbles of Bliss

Floating dreams in vibrant hue,
Laughter bubbles, joy in view,
In the sun, they shimmer bright,
Each one carries pure delight.

Children chase in carefree mirth,
Chasing joy upon the earth,
Bubbles pop, but still they sing,
In their hearts, the joy they bring.

Brushstrokes of Elation

In vibrant hues, the day unfolds,
Joy paints the sky with strokes of gold.
Laughter spills from every heart,
As hope and dream refuse to part.

The canvas brightens with each smile,
Time pauses, though just for a while.
In the gallery of moments shared,
Elation whispers, love, and care.

The Kaleidoscope of Now

Fragments of color swirl and gleam,
Moments merge like a fleeting dream.
Every turn, a new surprise,
Life's mosaic beneath the skies.

Patterns shift in vibrant play,
Every second, a brand new way.
In the blink of an eye they twine,
A dance of light, yours and mine.

Laughter in the Breezes

Soft whispers through the gentle trees,
Laughter carries on the breeze.
Playful echoes fill the air,
A melody of joy to share.

Bright eyes sparkle, warmth surrounds,
In every heartbeat, laughter sounds.
Nature's joy in every frame,
Together, we become the same.

Sunlight Dancing on Water

Ripples shimmer, a golden song,
Sunlight spins where waters throng.
Each wave a story yet untold,
A ballet in the warm sunlight's hold.

The world reflects in glistening trails,
As laughter mingles with the gales.
Nature's waltz, so pure and free,
In this moment, just you and me.

Kites in the Open Sky

Bright kites soar on high,
Dancing with the breeze.
Colors blur and fly,
Creating dreams with ease.

Children shout with glee,
Chasing shadows near.
Laughter wild and free,
Echoes in the clear.

Strings that pull and reel,
Hearts entwined in flight.
Moments that we feel,
Adventure in the light.

As the sun dips low,
Kites descend with grace.
In twilight's soft glow,
A joyful, sweet embrace.

The Dance of Daisies

Daisies in a row,
Swaying in the sun.
Whispers soft and low,
Nature's dance begun.

Petals white and bright,
Crowned by golden hues.
Beneath the blue light,
They share morning news.

Bees hum all around,
Joyful in their flight.
In this magic ground,
Life feels pure and right.

Underneath the trees,
Soft shadows cascade.
The gentle breeze sees,
Daisies serenade.

Radiant Threads of Connection

Lives woven so tight,
In a tapestry.
Threads of shared delight,
Stitch our history.

Hearts beat in a tune,
Echoes from the past.
Beneath the full moon,
Memories are cast.

Stories intertwine,
Like vines in the air.
Each moment a sign,
Of the love we share.

In this vibrant quilt,
Every patch a tale,
From the dreams we built,
To the winds that sail.

Coraline's Daydream

In a world so bright,
Coraline will roam.
Through the door of light,
She finds a new home.

Adventures await,
In shadows and light.
Secrets on each plate,
With wonders in sight.

Daring and so bold,
She treads unknown paths.
With courage to hold,
And face all the wrath.

In her heart she knows,
It's never just play.
For with each door's close,
A new dawn will sway.

A Cup Overflowing

In morning light, a cup does shine,
Filled with warmth, a love divine.
Each drop a joy, a sweet embrace,
A moment shared, a tranquil space.

With laughter rich, the spirits soar,
As flavors blend, we crave for more.
In every sip, a story's told,
Of life and dreams, and hearts so bold.

Together we toast, both near and far,
Under the glow of a radiant star.
A cup overflowing, our hearts ignite,
In cherished bonds, our souls take flight.

Footprints in the Sand

The waves recede, the shoreline bare,
Footprints left in the ocean's care.
A tale of journeys, joys, and fears,
Washed away by laughter and tears.

Beneath the sun, we walked as one,
Chasing shadows, embracing fun.
Where footprints linger, memories remain,
In gentle whispers, love's sweet refrain.

With every tide, new paths appear,
Yet in my heart, you are always near.
Together we tread, through thick and thin,
In the sand of time, our story begins.

Glimmers of a Grateful Heart

In twilight's hush, a moment gleams,
A heart filled with hope, a treasure of dreams.
Each breath a gift, each smile a start,
In life's embrace, glimmers depart.

Through trials faced, and joy embraced,
We find our light in love interlaced.
With gratitude penned on every page,
A story of growth, a soulful stage.

In silence shared, we find our peace,
From worldly burdens, we seek release.
Glimmers of light in every part,
Shine brightly forth from a grateful heart.

A Canvas of Cheer

Brush in hand, I paint the day,
With colors bright that dance and sway.
Each stroke a smile, each hue a laugh,
A masterpiece born from love's sweet craft.

The sun's embrace, the sky so blue,
In every shade, memories new.
Joy we can share, hope we can feel,
On this canvas, our hearts reveal.

With laughter's echo, and kindness near,
We fill each corner with joy and cheer.
A canvas alive, where wishes soar,
Together we create, forevermore.

Dancing in Sunlight

Golden rays embrace the ground,
Frolicking shadows all around.
Children's laughter fills the air,
Joyful moments, free from care.

Leaves are swaying in the breeze,
Nature's dance among the trees.
Hearts are light, our spirits soar,
Sunlit pathways, we explore.

Every step a fleeting dream,
In the warmth, we laugh and beam.
Underneath this sky so bright,
We're alive, in pure delight.

Whispers of Laughter

In the quiet of the night,
Softened giggles take to flight.
Echoes of a playful jest,
Friendship's warmth, we are blessed.

Moonbeams dance upon the wall,
Little secrets, we enthrall.
Stories shared in gentle tones,
Whispers turn to happy groans.

Under stars, we find our cheer,
Moments cherished, oh so dear.
With each laugh, a bond we weave,
In this joy, we both believe.

A Tapestry of Smiles

Colors blend, both bright and bold,
Threads of joy, a story told.
Stitched together, heart by heart,
In this art, we'll never part.

Each smile casts away the gray,
Radiant hues, we find our way.
Together, every stitch we make,
A tapestry, no hearts will break.

In laughter's glow, we intertwine,
With every shared moment, we shine.
Bold and beautiful, we compile,
Creating life, a tapestry of smiles.

The Color of Happiness

Brush strokes of a vibrant hue,
Sparkling skies, a brilliant view.
Fields of gold and oceans blue,
In this palette, dreams come true.

Every sunrise paints the day,
With colors bright to light our way.
Joyful hearts in every shade,
In this canvas, love is laid.

Moments captured, bright and rare,
In each color, we lay bare.
The essence of what we feel,
The color of happiness is real.

Sparkling Brew of Laughter

In a cup of joy, we blend,
Laughter bubbles, heart to mend.
Every sip a giggle bright,
Sparkling moments, pure delight.

Friends gather round, stories flow,
With every joke, the love does grow.
A toast to life, so warm and free,
In this brew, we find our glee.

Like bubbles dancing in the air,
Each laugh a spark, a twinkling flare.
Together we chase worries away,
Sipping smiles, come what may.

So raise your cups, let spirits soar,
In this brew, we're never poor.
For in laughter, we've found our thread,
A sparkling brew to be widespread.

Echoes of Delight

In the garden, laughter rings,
Echoes dance on joyous wings.
Each petal shares a whispered tale,
Of sunlit days and breezy sail.

Children's giggles fill the air,
A melody so light and rare.
With every step, the joy ignites,
In vibrant days and starlit nights.

The rustling leaves, a gentle cheer,
With every sound, the heart draws near.
Nature sings, a sweet embrace,
Echoes of delight in every space.

So let us wander, hand in hand,
In laughter's arms, we'll make our stand.
For in these echoes, love's in sight,
A symphony of pure delight.

Serenade of Serendipity

A chance encounter, magic's thread,
In unexpected paths, we tread.
Whispers soft, the hearts align,
A serenade, the stars entwine.

With every turn, surprises bloom,
In life's rich tapestry, no gloom.
A gentle nudge, a smile shared,
In serendipity, we're declared.

Moments fleeting, yet so sublime,
In laughter's dance, we beat time.
Let's celebrate the joy of chance,
In life's sweet song, let's take a dance.

So if you find a spark so bright,
Hold on tight, embrace the light.
For in each twist, life's magic grows,
A serenade that softly glows.

The Magic of Simple Things

In sunlight's warm and golden ray,
A simple flower leads the way.
Each gentle breeze, a tender kiss,
In quiet moments, we find bliss.

A cozy nook, a book to read,
In every page, our hearts are freed.
The warmth of tea, a soothing blend,
In simple joys, our souls transcend.

A child's sweet laugh, a friend's embrace,
In each small act, we find our place.
With grateful hearts, we take a swing,
In life's orchestra, we play and sing.

So cherish these amidst the rush,
In simple things, there's no need to hush.
For magic lies where we can cling,
To life's sweet song, the joy they bring.

Blossoming with the Dawn

As golden rays greet the day,
The flowers stretch, ready to play.
Soft whispers of the morning breeze,
Awakening life among the trees.

Colors dance in the gentle light,
Nature's canvas, pure delight.
Every petal, a story untold,
Blossoming dreams in hues so bold.

The sun climbs high, a radiant sphere,
Chasing away the night's last fear.
With each moment, hope is born,
In a world that sings of the dawn.

Together we bask in the glow,
Finding joy in the seeds we sow.
In every heart, let beauty thrive,
As we embrace the day, alive.

Strings of Shared Laughter

In the garden, we gather near,
With stories shared, our hearts cheer.
Each laugh a thread in our warm quilt,
Connecting us all with love's sweet tilt.

Bright moments spin like golden thread,
Carrying joy as we tread.
In the echoes, our spirits align,
Crafting memories, pure and divine.

Through ups and downs, we stand so bold,
Our laughter, a treasure more than gold.
Every giggle a gentle embrace,
A melody sweet, time can't erase.

With every chuckle, bonds grow strong,
In this symphony where we belong.
Together we dance, time feels so right,
In the strings of laughter, pure delight.

Memories That Make Us Shine

In the heart's vault, treasures lie,
Reflections of the days gone by.
Moments captured in time's embrace,
Light up our paths, fill empty space.

A giggle, a tear, a whisper soft,
Each memory lifts us, carries us aloft.
Stored in the chambers of our soul,
A tapestry woven, making us whole.

Golden sunsets and starlit skies,
Echoing laughter, the softest sighs.
In every heartbeat, a story spins,
Memories alive, where love begins.

We cherish the past, though it may wane,
For in our hearts, it will remain.
These moments, vibrant, forever entwined,
Shimmering brightly, making us shine.

A Journey Through Radiance

In every step, the light guides me,
Through valleys deep and mountains free.
With every dawn, a new chance to grow,
And bask in the radiance that we know.

Stars above, painting the night,
Illuminating dreams with silver light.
Each moment a treasure, a path to tread,
With hope as our compass, we're gently led.

The sun smiles down, embracing the way,
As we wander through night into day.
With hearts aglow and spirits bright,
We journey onward, bathed in light.

Together we venture, hand in hand,
Through a world that sings, vibrant and grand.
In the glow of love, forever we'll be,
A journey through radiance, wild and free.

Dancing Through the Feathered Fields

In fields of green, the feathers fly,
Children laugh as clouds drift by.
With every step, the flowers sway,
In nature's dance, we find our play.

The sunbeams kiss the dewy grass,
As twinkles in the air amass.
Joyful hearts, both young and old,
In feathered fields, our dreams unfold.

Golden Threads of Delight

Threads of gold weave through the light,
Binding wishes, pure and bright.
With every stitch, a story spun,
Crafting joy beneath the sun.

Moments glimmer, soft and rare,
In every smile, a whispered prayer.
Golden threads of hope unite,
Binding love in pure delight.

Glimmers of Glee

In the dawn, the world awakes,
With glimmers of joy that laughter makes.
Every heartbeat, a song of cheer,
Whispers of happiness drawing near.

Like stars that twinkle in the night,
Each flicker brings the heart to light.
Glimmers of glee, they softly play,
Filling our souls with warmth each day.

The Art of Serendipity

A chance encounter, a serendipity,
Moments unfold with sweet simplicity.
Paths entwine in a dance so free,
Guided by fate, just you and me.

In the whispers of the gentle breeze,
We find magic among the trees.
With open hearts, we embrace the chance,
This is the art of life's true dance.

Embraces Under Soft Canopies

Beneath the branches, shadows play,
Whispers of leaves guide the day.
In gentle arms, we find our grace,
Nature's touch, a warm embrace.

Sunbeams dance in filtered light,
Peace envelops, hearts take flight.
Under sky, our laughter spills,
Moments cherished, time stands still.

With every sigh, the world turns slow,
In this haven, love can grow.
Soft canopies shelter our dreams,
In each glance, a story gleams.

Together we weave, a tapestry bright,
In the shade, everything feels right.
Forever bound by this connection,
Embraced in nature's sweet reflection.

The Lightness of Being

Floating softly on a breeze,
Moments captured with such ease.
Every heartbeat sings a song,
In this joy, we both belong.

Joyful laughter fills the air,
Weightless dreams without a care.
Seeking beauty in the small,
Life is lovely, after all.

Wandering paths of golden hues,
In each step, a chance to choose.
The sun sets low, yet hope prevails,
Guiding us on vibrant trails.

Lightness cradles each desire,
Hearts ignited with pure fire.
In this dance, we share the space,
The lightness of being finds its place.

Hearts in Bloom

In the garden where love grows,
Petals open, soft and slow.
Colors burst in every hue,
Hearts in bloom, forever true.

The fragrance lifts with morning dew,
Promises whispered, fresh as new.
Each embrace, a seed we sow,
In the warmth, our passions flow.

Gentle winds caress the sight,
Filling souls with pure delight.
Together weaving dreams anew,
Hearts in bloom, just me and you.

With every star that lights the night,
Love's creation feels so right.
Together we'll make flowers thrive,
In this garden, we're alive.

Celebrating Shimmering Time

Moments twinkle, soft and bright,
Fragments glimmer in the night.
Each second holds a story dear,
In shimmering time, love draws near.

The clock ticks softly, hearts align,
Memories linger, sweetly shine.
Laughter echoes through the years,
Celebrating joy, tempered tears.

Every glance is woven tight,
In the tapestry of light.
Cherished whispers in the air,
In this dance, we find repair.

So let us toast to days gone by,
To fleeting moments that never die.
Celebrating lives entwined,
In shimmering time, our hearts remind.

Smiles That Span the Universe

Across the sky, a gentle glow,
Laughter dances, soft and slow.
In every heart, the light we share,
A cosmic bond, beyond compare.

From distant stars to oceans wide,
Smiles travel far, no need to hide.
In every glance, a spark ignites,
Connecting souls on starry nights.

Through every storm, we find our way,
Together strong, we will not sway.
In universe vast, we rise above,
Bound by the threads of endless love.

So let us beam, as dawn unfolds,
In smiles that span, the stories told.
A tapestry of joy we weave,
In every moment, we believe.

Moments Wrapped in Warmth

In the quiet, shadows play,
Whispers of the end of day.
Cocoa steaming, laughter shared,
In these moments, hearts are bared.

A blanket's touch, a fire's glow,
In gentle warmth, our spirits grow.
Through fleeting time, we pause and breathe,
In love's embrace, we find reprieve.

Each tick of time, a treasure dear,
In simple joys, we gather near.
A glance, a smile, a soft caress,
Wrapped in warmth, we feel so blessed.

So hold these moments, let them stay,
In memory's book, they softly play.
With every heartbeat, we will find,
The warmth of love, forever kind.

The Joy of Simple Pleasures

A morning bloom, the scent of rain,
In quiet moments, joy's refrain.
A robin sings, the world awakes,
In simple things, our spirit stakes.

A book held close, the pages worn,
In whispered tales, new dreams are born.
Sunset hues, a canvas bright,
In golden hours, we find our light.

A hand to hold, a laugh to share,
In fleeting time, our hearts laid bare.
Each humble act, a snapshot clear,
In joyful whispers, love draws near.

So cherish moments, simple, sweet,
In daily life, let's find our beat.
For joy resides in what we do,
In simple pleasures, ever true.

Spheres of Radiant Energy

In every heart, a spark ignites,
A sphere of love through endless nights.
We pulse with joy, as galaxies spin,
Together strong, let the light in.

The sun that rises, the moon that glows,
In nature's dance, our spirit flows.
Amidst the stars, our dreams take flight,
In vibrant hues, we chase the light.

Each breath we take, a sacred gift,
In cosmic tides, we find our lift.
As spheres of energy, we unite,
Spreading warmth, dispelling fright.

So let us shine, with all our might,
In unity, we'll face the night.
For in our cores, the universe sways,
In radiant energy, let us blaze.

The Sweetness of Being Present

In the quiet moments shared,
Time slips softly through our hands.
A glance, a smile, gentle and rare,
Life's beauty, like golden sands.

Breathe in the love that's all around,
Feel the warmth of hearts that meet.
In the now, pure joy is found,
Every heartbeat feels so sweet.

Let worries fade, like distant dreams,
Embrace the magic, let it flow.
In presence, life is more than seems,
In this stillness, let us grow.

Together we weave memories bright,
Threads of laughter, colors bold.
In this moment, everything feels right,
Hand in hand, our stories told.

Glowing Gatherings

Under the stars, we come alive,
Laughter echoing through the night.
In these moments, we truly thrive,
Hearts aglow with shared delight.

Friends gathered 'round, spirits high,
Every story brings us near.
Beneath the vast and open sky,
We cherish every laugh and cheer.

With fires flickering, shadows dance,
Warmth wraps us like a soft embrace.
In this place, we take our chance,
To create memories time won't erase.

As dawn approaches, we'll hold tight,
To the magic we've woven here.
These glowing gatherings feel so right,
In our hearts, we'll keep them dear.

Echoes of Innocent Laughter

In the garden where dreams take flight,
Children's laughter fills the air.
Chasing shadows, pure delight,
Innocence beyond compare.

Tiny feet run wild and free,
Joy reflected in each small face.
Every giggle a melody,
In their hearts, a sacred space.

Time slows down as games unfold,
Imagination knows no bounds.
In every story brightly told,
The world is rich with joyful sounds.

As the sun begins to set,
Memories linger like sweet rain.
In echoes of laughter, we won't forget,
The purest joy, forever remains.

A Canvas of Bright Horizons

Brush strokes of orange, pink, and gold,
Sunrise paints the waking sky.
Each new day a story bold,
A canvas where dreams learn to fly.

In every corner, colors blend,
Hope unfurls like blossoming flowers.
With every dawn, life starts to mend,
Creating magic in our hours.

As shadows fade, possibilities spark,
The horizon calls us to explore.
In the light, we leave our mark,
Chasing dreams we can't ignore.

With hearts open wide, we'll pave the way,
For new adventures, hand in hand.
On this canvas, come what may,
We'll paint a life that's truly grand.

The Dance of Delighted Souls

In twilight's gentle embrace, they sway,
Whispers of joy guide their way.
Stars twinkle bright in the deepening night,
Together they twirl, basking in light.

Laughter echoes, a melodious sound,
Each step they take, firmly bound.
Hearts intertwine in a rhythmic beat,
In this sacred moment, they are complete.

Time drifts softly, a cherished theme,
In this dance, they continue to dream.
With every spin, a story unfolds,
Of love and delight, as the night molds.

As dawn approaches, shadows retreat,
They hold onto joy, their hearts skip a beat.
A dance of souls, forever entwined,
In the echoes of laughter, solace they find.

Frolics in the Meadow's Heart

Beneath the blue, where wildflowers grow,
Children chase sunlight, laughing in tow.
Butterflies flutter, colors so bright,
A symphony dances in pure delight.

Tall grass sways to a playful tune,
Breezes carry dreams beneath the noon.
The babbling brook joins in with glee,
Nature's chorus, wild and free.

Carefree spirits with hearts full of cheer,
Find joy in the moments held dear.
Every step taken, a leap, a bound,
In the meadow's heart, happiness found.

As the sun dips low, casting gold on the land,
They cherish the day, hand in hand.
With memories made, they twirl and spin,
The frolics of youth, where love begins.

A Parade of Sunlit Laughter

The morning breaks with a jubilant cheer,
Children gather, their voices clear.
With balloons and smiles, the streets alive,
A parade of laughter, where joy will thrive.

Sunny faces glow like the dawn,
Each step they take, a new magic drawn.
Well-worn paths echo with playful shouts,
As dreams emerge, dancing about.

Drummers beat out a lively tune,
In rhythm with hearts, they sway like the moon.
Colors cascade down the avenue,
A celebration vibrant, fresh as dew.

As the day wanes, they gather near,
Sharing in stories, laughter to cheer.
In this parade, love intertwines,
A tapestry woven through moments divine.

Lullabies of Pure Delight

Evening whispers a soothing song,
Crickets chirp softly, all night long.
Stars peek out, twinkling with grace,
In a world of dreams, they find their place.

Moonlight glimmers on the quiet stream,
Each ripple a note in a sweet dream.
With every hush, the heart takes flight,
Wrapped in lullabies of pure delight.

Gentle breezes carry tales from afar,
Of love's embrace, like a guiding star.
As eyelids droop and dreams swirl around,
In the echoes of night, peace is found.

In slumber's arms, they drift away,
To realms where joy and laughter play.
In this quietude, they hear the call,
Lullabies whispered, embracing all.

Whirlwinds of Bliss

In fields where wildflowers sway,
Joy dances with the breeze,
Laughter echoes, bright and free,
In nature's arms, we find ease.

Clouds whisper secrets up high,
Sunlight spills like golden rain,
Hearts twirl in sweet harmony,
In these moments, we remain.

Dreams spin like a child's kite,
Carried high on hopes so light,
Twisting, turning, pure delight,
In whirlwinds, our souls take flight.

With every breath, we embrace,
The magic found in life's chase,
In blissful storms, we find grace,
Together lost in this warm space.

The Magic of Little Wins

In morning light, we rise anew,
With coffee warmth held in our hands,
A smile shared, a simple truth,
The magic of small, bold stands.

A friendly word can lift a day,
A gesture small, yet deeply kind,
In wins so small, we find our way,
In joyous moments intertwined.

Each tiny step is progress made,
In little joys, our spirits soar,
With every laugh, a bond is laid,
In victories, we rejoice and more.

Count the blessings, one by one,
Celebrate what's often missed,
In life's grand game, we have our fun,
The magic lies in each small twist.

Starlit Conversations

Underneath a blanket of stars,
Whispers dance upon the night,
Secrets shared from near and far,
Hearts connect in soft moonlight.

Time slows down, we lose our cares,
In the cosmos, dreams collide,
Moments captured, love declares,
In starlit frames, we confide.

The universe listens close,
As galaxies spin and glide,
In these talks, we find the most,
A tapestry of souls beside.

Each twinkle holds a shared sigh,
In laughter, dreams take flight,
Together we reach for the sky,
In starlit conversations, pure delight.

Unveiling the Color of Wellness

In the morning, soft and bright,
Nature sings a healing song,
Amidst the colors, pure and right,
Each hue reminds us where we belong.

Green whispers of life anew,
The blue of peace wraps us tight,
Yellow beams of warmth shine through,
In this canvas, our spirits take flight.

With every breath, let love flow,
In colors bright, we paint our way,
Wellness blooms, a gentle show,
In vibrant shades, we find our stay.

Embrace the palette, rich and bold,
In every moment, joy unfolds,
As we unveil the colors of soul,
In wellness, we find life's gold.

Shimmering Smiles and Friendly Grins

In the sun, we laugh and play,
Whispers of joy come out to stay.
Every giggle, a spark so bright,
Shimmering smiles, pure delight.

Together in a world so grand,
Hands held tight, we make our stand.
Friendship blooms like flowers in spring,
With friendly grins, our hearts take wing.

Beneath the stars, our secrets share,
With every moment, love's sweet flare.
Chasing dreams both wild and free,
In this dance, just you and me.

As daylight fades, our smiles remain,
A tapestry woven with joy and pain.
Through every trial, we find our way,
In shimmering smiles, we forever stay.

Chasing Rainbows Beneath the Sky

Underneath the azure dome,
We wander, far away from home.
Chasing colors bright and bold,
In nature's arms, our stories unfold.

Every step a new surprise,
Painting dreams in open skies.
Laughter chasing shadows near,
Finding treasures, year by year.

Clouds may drift and storms may blow,
Yet through the trials, we always grow.
Hand in hand, we brave the gust,
In faith and hope, we place our trust.

Together, we will see the end,
With every turn, our hearts transcend.
For in the hues of life's embrace,
Chasing rainbows, we find our place.

Bubbles of Pure Happiness

Floating dreams in a world of cheer,
Bubbles rise, laughter to hear.
Each one holds a wish so bright,
Dancing in sunlight, pure delight.

Giggles fill the playful air,
Creating magic everywhere.
In simple joys, we find the rise,
A universe behind our eyes.

With every pop, a secret set free,
A bond that whispers, 'You and me.'
Together we chase the fleeting thrill,
In bubbles of joy, our hearts stand still.

So let us blow and watch them soar,
In every bubble, love to explore.
In this moment, all cares depart,
Bubbles of happiness fill the heart.

Memories Painted with Light

In the canvas of days gone by,
Golden memories never die.
Each moment a stroke, vivid and clear,
Painted with love, forever near.

Time slips like sand through our hands,
Yet in our hearts, the love still stands.
With every sunrise, new dreams ignite,
As memories glow, painted with light.

Whispers of laughter, echoes of past,
Moments cherished, forever cast.
Through the lens of time, we gaze anew,
In every hue, our bond is true.

So let us weave our tales tonight,
Underneath the stars, so bright.
For in this tapestry, we find our fate,
Memories painted, love creates.

A Carousel of Memories

Spinning gently, time holds tight,
Colors blur in soft daylight.
Whispers of laughter, shadows cast,
Moments linger, echoes last.

Each smile a frame, a fleeting glance,
In the dance of chance, we take our stance.
Against the whirl, we shout our dreams,
In this circle, nothing's as it seems.

Childhood whispers, secrets shared,
In every turn, we felt so dared.
Treasured glimpses, we hold so dear,
On this ride, we conquer fear.

Round and round, the stories flow,
In joyful hues, we learn and grow.
With every spin, we find our place,
In this carousel, we embrace grace.

Twilight Laughter

As daylight dims, the stars appear,
In twilight's veil, laughter draws near.
Chasing shadows, we run and play,
   Under hues of pink and gray.

The sky aglow, the world in hush,
In the fading light, feelings rush.
Whispers of love ride on the breeze,
   In this moment, hearts find ease.

Glimmers of joy in each small glance,
   Under the spell of twilight's dance.
Sharing secrets, we dream so wide,
   In the magic where hopes abide.

With every chuckle, our spirits soar,
In the twilight's glow, we yearn for more.
Embracing life, with hearts so bright,
   Together we weave through the night.

Joy in the Tickle of Raindrops

Pitter-patter on rooftops play,
Nature's drum in a vast array.
With every drop, the world transforms,
In this dance, our spirit warms.

Children laugh, splashing feet,
In puddles shallow, joy's retreat.
Umbrellas bloom like flowers bright,
Celebrating life in pure delight.

The sky releases a fresh embrace,
Each raindrop tells a sweet new grace.
We twirl and spin, abandon worry,
In raindrops, we find no hurry.

So let it rain, let the waters flow,
In nature's gift, our hearts will glow.
For in each drop, love's spark ignites,
In the rhythm of life, pure delight.

The Sweet Surrender of Happiness

Soft as a whisper, sweet as the sun,
Happiness lingers, a warm, gentle fun.
In every heartbeat, a rhythm we find,
With open arms, we embrace the unwind.

Chasing the light, we dance so free,
Moments captured, just you and me.
In laughter shared, worries take flight,
In the warmth of love, all feels right.

Dreams woven gently, threads of delight,
In the tapestry of life, we unite.
With every smile, we paint the skies,
In the sweet surrender, our spirit flies.

Let the world pass by, we're here to stay,
In this dance of joy, come what may.
For in each heartbeat, we truly see,
The sweet surrender, our souls set free.

Playful Shadows at Dusk

Shadows dance beneath the tree,
Whispers float on a gentle breeze.
Children laugh, chasing the light,
As day bids farewell to the night.

Colors blend in a soft embrace,
The sun dips low, a golden trace.
Fireflies blink like stars on the ground,
Evening's calm, a magical sound.

Footprints left in the fading sun,
Tales of laughter, joy, and fun.
The world slows down, a perfect scene,
As twilight wraps us in a dream.

In this moment, time stands still,
Hearts are full, and spirits thrill.
Playful shadows, soft and light,
Guide us gently into the night.

A Symphony of Smiles

In a world of vibrant hues,
Each smile sings a joyful muse.
Friendships bloom like flowers bright,
Chasing darkness, bringing light.

Laughter twirls in the air,
A melody, sweet and rare.
Every glance, a note so pure,
In this symphony, we find sure.

Together, we dance through the day,
Making worries fade away.
Sharing secrets, dreams, and cheer,
Building bonds that persevere.

A radiant chorus of delight,
Echoes softly through the night.
With every smile, we create,
A harmony that can't wait.

Bliss in Every Breath

Inhale deeply, pure and clear,
Life's sweet essence drawing near.
With each breath, feel the glow,
Nature's rhythm, gentle flow.

Moments linger, soft and kind,
In the stillness, peace we find.
A spark of joy in the mundane,
Whispers of hope, a soft refrain.

Time unfolds in quiet grace,
Each heartbeat finding its place.
With gratitude, we exist,
Embracing life, a tender kiss.

In every breath, a gift we hold,
Stories of love and dreams untold.
Bliss envelops, warm and light,
Guiding hearts into the night.

Savoring the Sweetest Hours

As the clock ticks by so slow,
We find magic in the glow.
Moments linger, soft and sweet,
Time dances to a gentle beat.

With every sip of morning tea,
We gather joy, just you and me.
Sunshine spills through window panes,
Washing away our lingering pains.

Laughter echoes, fills the space,
In these hours, we find our place.
Stories shared, memories dear,
Whispers of love that draw us near.

As day fades into twilight's hue,
We'll savor what is warm and true.
In these moments, life empowers,
Together, we embrace sweet hours.

Waves of Bright Serenity

Beneath the sunlit skies,
The waves dance and play.
Whispers of the ocean,
Carry worries away.

Soft sands beneath our feet,
Gentle breezes sigh.
In the harmony of nature,
We learn to breathe and fly.

Seashells tell of journeys,
Treasures from afar.
Each wave a sweet reminder,
Of dreams like morning stars.

With every rising tide,
Our spirits start to soar.
Embracing waves of brightness,
We seek forevermore.

Footsteps on the Path of Joy

Each step leads us onward,
Footprints in the dust.
With a heart that's open wide,
In joy, we place our trust.

Sunlight filters through trees,
Nature's warm embrace.
Every laugh and every smile,
Leaves a lasting trace.

Candles flicker brightly,
In the warmth of our sphere.
Together we march forward,
With love that draws us near.

In the rhythm of our journey,
Every moment's sweet.
On this path of joy, my friend,
Life's melody's complete.

A Tapestry of Glorious Memories

Threads of laughter woven,
Colors bright and bold.
In each stitch, a story,
Of times we have retold.

Moments strung together,
Like pearls upon a string.
A tapestry of memories,
In our hearts they sing.

From quiet, gentle whispers,
To echoes of the past,
Each memory a treasure,
A bond that's meant to last.

Let us gather 'round the hearth,
Share tales both old and new.
In this tapestry of life,
Our love will shine right through.

Glowing Faces in the Twilight

As day gives way to night,
Soft glimmers start to rise.
Glowing faces all around,
Reflecting starry skies.

In the hush of twilight,
Whispers fill the air.
Stories shared and laughter,
In friendship's tender care.

The world slows down its pace,
As shadows softly blend.
Each moment we gather close,
A treasure without end.

With glowing faces shining,
We embrace the fading light.
In the warmth of togetherness,
We're safe until the night.

A Daydream in Full Bloom

In the garden where thoughts go,
Colors swirl like a soft breeze,
Whispers of petals gently flow,
As time drips with sweet ease.

Beneath the sun's warm embrace,
Dreams dance upon the ground,
With every thought, we find our place,
In joys that know no bound.

The world fades, it becomes a blur,
Lost in a melody so fine,
Even a hint of doubt can stir,
Yet hope is a cherished sign.

Awake or lost in a dream's bloom,
Hearts flutter like the butterfly's wing,
In each petal, there's room for gloom,
But the light soon emerges to sing.

Petals of Positivity

Each petal holds a promise fair,
Bright colors shining in the light,
Crafted from dreams we dare,
They dance in the breeze, taking flight.

With every bloom, a hope unfolds,
Warming hearts in winter's chill,
A tale of joy silently told,
Echoing love, a soft thrill.

In laughter, we sow the seeds,
Cultivating warmth in each heart,
Finding strength in life's small deeds,
A garden where we all take part.

Petals fall like whispered cheer,
Each one carries vibrant grace,
In the silence, dreams draw near,
Painting smiles on every face.

Echoing Happiness

In the stillness of the night,
A laughter lingers on the air,
A melody of pure delight,
Cascading joy beyond compare.

The trees sway, their branches sing,
In harmony with the moon's glow,
Each echo, a cherished thing,
Reminding us of love's flow.

Moments blend like colors bright,
Painting memories with sweet sound,
In the echoes, we find our light,
Lost in happiness profound.

With every heartbeat, joy will swell,
Resonating through the gloom,
In this rhythm, we shall dwell,
Forever wrapped in happiness' bloom.

Whirling Through the Seasons

Each season spins a tale so sweet,
Winter's chill and summer's blaze,
With autumn's gold beneath our feet,
And spring's embrace a warm amaze.

Blossoms swirl, a dance divine,
Carried through the soft spring air,
Time whispers secrets, like fine wine,
As colors change, we roam with care.

Summer's sun invites us near,
Days stretch long, hearts open wide,
In laughter laughed, no room for fear,
We bloom in joy, our worlds collide.

With autumn's brush, leaves gently fall,
Painting pathways with hues so bright,
While winter wraps the earth in shawl,
We find warmth in each starry night.

Dancing Shadows

In twilight's glow, they sway and dance,
Whispers of night, a mystic trance.
Beneath the trees, they leap and glide,
In silent rhythms, shadows abide.

A flicker here, a shimmer there,
Echoing dreams in the cool night air.
Footsteps soft on the forest floor,
They twirl and spin, forevermore.

The moonlight casts, a silver sheen,
Of tangled forms, and sights unseen.
With each soft breeze, they curl and fade,
In the warm embrace, of evening's jade.

And when dawn breaks, they take their leave,
Carried away, on webs they weave.
Yet in our hearts, their dance remains,
A haunting melody in gentle refrains.

Starlit Giggles

Under a veil of twinkling lights,
Soft laughs escape, in joyful nights.
Each star above, a wink and grin,
As friendship blooms, and hearts begin.

We chase the dreams, so high and bright,
In stardust trails, we take our flight.
Every giggle, a spark of glee,
In this vast sky, just you and me.

Moonbeams play on our carefree souls,
Painting our paths, where laughter rolls.
With whispered secrets, and tales once told,
We weave our stories, brave and bold.

And as the night begins to wane,
Our starlit joy, forever remains.
In cosmic warmth, we'll always shine,
Bound by the giggles, yours and mine.

Raindrops and Rainbows

Raindrops dance on the window pane,
In gentle rhythms, a sweet refrain.
Each drop a story, a tale of grace,
As clouds embrace, the sun's soft face.

With every splash, the world awakes,
Nature sings, as the earth partakes.
Colors emerge from the storm's embrace,
A vibrant arc in sky's wide space.

Puddles form, reflections shine,
A mirror of dreams, so pure, divine.
Children laugh, splashing feet,
In this watery world, life feels complete.

Then comes the sun, casting rain's glow,
Painting the skies, a radiant show.
With hope renewed, we chase the light,
In raindrops and rainbows, hearts take flight.

The Symphony of Smiles

In every corner, a smile awaits,
A silent song that love creates.
With gentle curves, and eyes that gleam,
It weaves a magic, a tender dream.

From strangers met, to friends so dear,
Each grin a note, that we can hear.
With laughter shared, we harmonize,
As joy unfolds beneath the skies.

In crowded places, or quiet streets,
The symphony plays, as heartbeats meet.
Every chuckle, a bright refrain,
Of warmth that lingers, like softest rain.

So let us gather, and let us sing,
For smiles are treasures, that love can bring.
In this sweet symphony, we find our way,
With every smile, a brand new day.

Whispers of a Happy Heart

In quiet moments, joy takes flight,
A gentle breeze on a warm moonlight.
Sweet laughter dances, light as air,
Whispers promise love is everywhere.

Soft petals bloom in colors bright,
Each heartbeat sings, a pure delight.
In every glance, a story starts,
Together woven, our hopeful hearts.

Through golden fields and starry skies,
Every glance speaks, no need for lies.
A joyful spirit, bold and free,
Embracing life, just you and me.

With every dawn, a chance to play,
In whispered dreams, we find our way.
In shared moments, joy imparts,
The sweetest songs of happy hearts.

Radiant Echoes of Laughter

Beneath the sun, we chase the day,
In joyful giggles, worries sway.
Echoes linger, laughter's tune,
With every moment, we bloom like June.

Through winding paths, our spirits soar,
Found in friendship, we seek for more.
Every shadow holds a play,
Radiant echoes light our way.

In timeless tales, we carve our name,
Each joke shared, a flickering flame.
United souls, we build and dream,
In laughter's grasp, the world can gleam.

So let us sing, let voices rise,
With radiant hearts, let's touch the skies.
Through joy, we find our sweetest art,
In echoes, we discover our heart.

The Blossom of Cheerful Days

Each morning brings a new surprise,
A world awash in vibrant skies.
Like flowers blooming, hearts embrace,
In the gentle warmth, we find our place.

The laughter spills like morning dew,
With every breath, the joy feels new.
In cheerful days, we walk as one,
A journey bright beneath the sun.

As seasons change, we intertwine,
In every moment, your hand in mine.
Together dancing, come what may,
In blossoms' glow, we find our way.

With open hearts, we greet the light,
Embracing life, our spirits bright.
In every smile, the beauty stays,
The blossom blooms in cheerful days.

Moments Wrapped in Sunshine

In golden rays, our laughter starts,
Wrapped in warmth, we share our hearts.
Each fleeting moment, bright and clear,
In sunshine's glow, we cast out fear.

With every step, we chase the light,
Painting memories, pure and bright.
In joyful whispers, dreams take wing,
In sunny days, we find our spring.

Dancing shadows play on ground,
In every heartbeat, love is found.
Moments treasured, soft and sweet,
Wrapped in sunshine, life's true treat.

So hand in hand, we roam the day,
With open hearts, we laugh and play.
In brightest hours, our joy we shine,
Wrapped in sunshine, forever divine.

Milton Keynes UK
Ingram Content Group UK Ltd.
UKHW051811101024
449294UK00007BA/58